Before You Marry...

Ask The

TOUGH

Questions

Before You Marry...

Ask The

TOUGH

Questions

by
Susan S. Levine

ISBN: 0-75960-790-7

This book is printed on acid free paper.

1stBooks – rev. 1/11/01

Acknowledgments

I would like to thank everyone who helped to make this book a reality. Special thanks go to my mother Virginia, my sister Emily, my brothers Rolt and Tom, and my uncle Phil for their support and willingness to put up with me. Even though they have no choice. :-)

To A.L. DeArmond, I extend my gratitude and appreciation for his outstanding editorial guidance. His enthusiasm and expertise made this book what it is.

Thanks also to Rebecca Lake, for her assistance in getting this book to print.

Dedication

This book is dedicated, with
all my love, to my son David,
who had the hardest job of all,
living with me while I was working.
Thanks, big guy.

Disclaimer

This author is not a marriage counselor, and the questions and ideas presented may not agree with opinions of those in the field. The suggestions in this book may not be suitable to all readers. The author and/or publisher disclaim any liability, loss, or risk incurred directly or indirectly as a result of reading and applying the contents of this book.

Table of Contents

Women's Questions

Sex - Either Partner

Men's Questions

Women's Questions

Personal Characteristics - Either Partner

Money - Either Partner

Men's Questions

Women's Questions

Family - Either Partner

Men's Questions

Women's Questions

Career - Either Partner

Men's Questions

Women's Questions

Health - Either Partner

Faith - Either Partner

Politics - Either Partner

Common Interests - Either Partner

Little Domestic Conflicts - Either Partner

Personal Behaviors And Habits - Either Partner

Women's Questions

In-Laws - Either Partner

Friends and Socializing - Either Partner

Remarriage - Either Partner

Introduction

You don't have to be engaged or in a serious relationship to have purchased this book. You may only be looking for an idea of the questions you should ask yourself and your partner (when you find him or her). Although the questions asked of you, as a male or female reader, are designed to help you find the answers you need, only you can know whether your personality and your partner's will make a marriage work.

During the time you are reading these pages, you are going to play a game of "pretend," just as you used to when you were a child. Imagine, if you will, that you are living in a different world. This world is very much like our current one, except for two important distinctions. First and foremost, there is NO legal divorce. None of any kind. No exceptions are made for spousal mistreatment or abuse. The words "till death do you part" are taken very seriously. Second, if you or your partner try to end the marriage illegally, you will be tried and imprisoned.

Sounds very frightening, doesn't it? You've just had your divorce safety net taken away, and a prison term if you decide to just leave the marriage if things don't work out as planned. But wouldn't this new, scary environment make you a lot more cautious? Would it not make you ask more questions, of yourself and your prospective spouse, as to whether you are suited to each other for the rest of your lives? If you discover–too late–the fact that your marriage does not live up to the dreams and expectations you had, you no longer have any exit. So, why not take the time to learn more about yourself and your partner now. You may discover things about each of you that could save you both from a mistake you would long regret. On the other hand, this process of discovery may either draw you closer together as a couple or end your relationship completely. Either way, you have nothing to lose in making this pre-marital journey as soon as possible.

There are twelve issues that feature most prominently during marriage: love, sex, money, family, career, religion, health, common interests, politics, personal behaviors and habits, in-laws, and friends. These issues, plus a few others, are addressed. Each chapter has questions applying to both partners, questions only for women, and those only for men. However, there are one or more sections without gender-specific questions. There is also a third section focusing on remarriage, since different questions arise when people marry for the second time. Issues such as children from the first marriage, property and assets must be examined prior to remarriage.

Prior to the issues chapters are sections focusing on the kind of marriage *(not the kind of wedding ceremony)* you want. There are the five common assumptions couples make and how to define the expectations you and your partner share about what should happen in *your* marriage. Read these sections over thoroughly, they are very important.

You may be wondering why there is no specific chapter concerning "communication" in this book. The reason is simple; this entire book is about how to communicate effectively with your partner and the issues that matter most to both of you. Some issues may apply directly to you; others may not. But you should go through the entire book, discovering along the way, the issues that can arise and talk about them with your partner before you get married.

What Kind Of Marriage Do You Want?

It is never too early to give some thought to this question. Knowing what you want or don't want in your marriage can be a very helpful guideline. Also, having a clearer picture of your own desires helps eliminate partners who would not meet your needs. This might be very confusing if you haven't thought out what you want beforehand. Where do you start? The first place might be your parents' marriage. What aspects of their relationship would you want to have–*or not*– in yours? Did they have a happy marriage, one that was miserable, or just somewhere in between?

Your next source for marriage research is your local bookstore, library, or both. Check out the section on marriage in your bookstore for books you might find interesting. If your funds are limited, take down the titles and authors of books you want, and ask your librarian if they either have the book available or if it could be ordered from another branch. At the end of this book, you'll find a suggested reading list, which could also help to get you started.

Whether you read only one book or a dozen, you cannot have too much of an education. Arming yourself with knowledge from objective and impartial sources often proves more valuable than relying on friends and family.

The well-intentioned folks who love you may have biases against or in favor of one form of marriage or another. Remember that regardless of the amount of materials you read, expanding your horizons on marriage is your primary objective. This is especially true if you are seriously considering matrimony. Once you know exactly what you do and don't want, discuss your thoughts with your partner. If you're not in a serious relationship right now, that's nothing to worry about. You can use the knowledge you're gaining to determine how compatible you and your next partner might be, when you're ready to begin dating again.

Although it may not be a great idea to discuss your perceptions of marriage on your first date, you don't have to wait long enough to become engaged before sharing your ideas. How else are you going to know if your new partner will feel the same as you, except by talking about it? You might even take things a step further by suggesting that he or she read the books you have. This would then allow for mutual discussion of your viewpoints based upon those books you both read.

What happens if your partner doesn't agree? You are faced with a tough decision; either compromise your ideals and settle for less, or end the current relationship. Neither of these will be easy choices. However, you have to ask yourself if it makes sense to abandon your values for someone who cannot or will not accept them. For example, what if you are a female reader who is in favor of a marriage more modern than traditional? Does your prospective husband want a woman who is more traditional? This does not mean the type of wedding; but

2

the marriage itself. If you have no idea what the difference is, you need to find out. And once you do, you'll be able to talk these differences over with him before you set any wedding date. Ultimately, the matrimonial decision is yours alone. Knowing what you want is the first step toward achievement.

Susan S. Levine

"Love is an ideal thing, marriage a real thing; a confusion of the real with the ideal never goes unpunished."

John Wolfgang von Goethe (1749-1832)

Assumptions That Couples Often Make

Prospective married couples often assume facts not in evidence. We have all heard what can happen when people "assume"–in each case it tends to make an "ass of u and me." Yet they continue to do this, even though it often leads to great unhappiness in both partners. Many couples make the following five assumptions without even being aware of it.

Assumption #1

Our expectations of married life are the same

Without taking the time to discuss with your prospective spouse what you each expect from one another after marriage, you're heading for a great deal of trouble. Many couples get so involved in preparing for "The Wedding," *(which is actually the beginning step of your marriage)* they lose sight of what they'll do after the ceremony and honeymoon are over. The next section, "Defining Your Expectations," provides an exercise allowing you both a chance at discovering what each expects of the other. Don't skip this one, it can make a very big difference in your marital future.

<u>Assumption #2</u>

Marriage will make all my personal problems go away

How deeply rooted are your problems is the question you must ask prior to deciding if marriage will be the cure-all you're hoping to find. Marriage is not a magic wand, where you wave it and all your problems disappear. The wedding is a ceremony joining two people, who have chosen to be together. But that's all it is; a ceremony. After it is over, you still have your problems to work through, in addition to the new problems your partner may be carrying around.

Make a list of the problems you're dealing with on your own now. This list should include only major concerns such as struggles with depression, single parenthood, substance addictions, and/or any other problems you feel are vitally important. Take a look at your list and ask yourself whether your spouse can realistically be depended upon, on their own, for elimination of these problems. Spouses may assist each other in finding ways to *help*, but cannot be expected to solve all the other person's problems *for* each other.

Assumption #3

My partner will make me happy

It is unrealistic to expect another person to be responsible for your happiness. And, doing so will in the future make your marriage a miserable existence for both of you. Also, it is highly likely you will not achieve the results you feel you should have. The concept of being happy has almost as many meanings as there are people. What may make one person happy could have exactly the opposite effect on the other person. You'll need to ask yourself some poignant questions.

Do you consider yourself a happy person in general? If not, is there any specific cause you're aware of for your depressed state? You shouldn't expect your partner to take on the responsibility of making you "happy," when he or she has no idea what is causing your unhappiness. Once you define the source or sources of your own unhappiness, you are better equipped to begin work on improving your personal outlook.

Assumption #4

My partner will change after marriage

Is there something about your partner you wish to change? Is it a significant change, such as a personal habit like substance addiction, or physical abuse destructive to both partners? Or simply a minor annoyance, such as the way your partner dresses? Either way you are headed for a big disappointment if you believe marriage alone will institute the changes desired.

You will need to identify what it is about your partner you believe needs changing. Assuming it's more of a "minor" fault, a frank discussion between you could effect the change desired. However for many, major issues such as their partner's choice of living, career, education or friends, aren't likely candidates to be affected greatly without considerable pain to both partners. These are only four serious issues. No doubt there are many others. If you don't like your partner's house or neighborhood for example, are you going to insist on him changing to a better place? Will you insist on this whether or not you both can afford it? What if he thinks it's good enough for him? Or maybe you don't care for her choice of career, since it might require long hours taking time away from your togetherness. A very important concern when you're first starting married life.

For example, one of you may have a home in good structural condition but needing cosmetic work. Doing a gradual redecorating project together could result in a home you can both be proud of. This is only one example of how the ability to compromise can work for you.

Any personal habits potentially harmful to you or your partner, such as any type of physical abuse, substance abuse and/or addiction, should be addressed *before* you get married. The chapter on personal habits deals with those in more detail. However, do not make the mistake of thinking that the simple ceremonial act of getting married will change them.

<u>Assumption #5</u>

My partner will not change after marriage

Almost everyone changes to some degree after marriage, although the differences might not happen immediately. The woman who was a "perfect 10" in terms of the body type her husband wanted may change after her first pregnancy. A man feeling on unequal ground intellectually could go back to school, get his college degree, and after that, a better job.

Nobody can stop the progress of personal change or growth. Sometimes, one partner can be very dependent on the other at the time they marry, but over time may outgrow this dependency, and become more able to stand on his or her own two feet. Although attaining a sense of independence is good, it can create a problem for the partner who provided the "leaning post" and may now have a feeling of being unneeded, or worse, unwanted.

This doesn't have to be a serious issue if the newly independent partner can assure the other that he or she is still loved, cherished and wanted. It is possible, however, that no matter what the partner does to reassure his or her spouse, it will be never be enough, and resentment of the change will persist and deepen. Make sure, before marrying, that you will be happy with each other, regardless of the physical or emotional changes that may happen as time passes.

Defining Your Expectations

Many marriages fail because one partner did not meet the expectations of the other. However, it doesn't help to learn what these expectations were after the damage has been done. Remember, for the duration of this book, you are living in a world of no legal divorce. You should have a clear understanding of your expectations and your partner's. So take the time to give your expectations some thought. Your partner should do the same. Write each one down, so they are clear in your mind. This exercise, for lack of a better word, requires an evening or two alone, when you can make a definitive and honest assessment.

By now, you are probably thinking how this is totally unromantic. You may feel you might as well list your assets and liabilities like a business partnership. But marriage *is* a partnership, and knowing what each partner expects of the other can make the difference between a loving relationship or a hostile one. If you both have conflicting expectations, you can try to work them out–or not–before marrying. Remember, the examples given below are just a few to help you get started on your own list. You may have one or two that are the same, and many that are entirely different.

Another point to remember is that your list may be shorter or longer. There is no minimum or maximum requirement.

11

Susan S. Levine

Man's Expectations

I expect my future wife to:
1.   Focus on the traditional roles of marriage
2.   Want to be a full-time mother
3.   Be an excellent cook
4.   Support my choice of career
5.   Be an enthusiastic partner in our sexual relationship
6.   Work to help support our lifestyle

Woman's Expectations

I expect my future husband to:
1.   Understand that I will not be the traditional wife his mother was
2.   Accept the idea that children will not be part of our marriage
3.   Be willing to cook or go out frequently, since I hate cooking
4.   Support my decision to stay in a career
5.   Be an exciting sexual partner
6.   Share in household chores and maintenance

     This is to give you an idea of what can happen when you go through this exercise. Each partner is going to read the other's list, and there is likely to be a spirited discussion when they find out what their partner's expectations are for them. No doubt each one may have believed their lists would be similar, if not identical. Look at the two lists; except for the last item on each, the others are in direct conflict. Let's examine the items on both lists carefully.

Item 1- Both partners have opposite expectations of the other. The man wants a more "traditional" wife, but is not specific about what his ideas of traditional are. The woman wants her future husband to understand, and accept, that she doesn't want to fill that role.

Item 2 - There is an enormous contrast here; he wants his future wife to be a mother, she wants him to accept a childless marriage.

Item 3 - He expects an excellent cook, she has made it clear she hates this job.

Item 4 - It is obvious that both partners want to stay in their respective careers, but it's possible that his could be very demanding, calling for long hours away from home. If he expects his wife to give up her career, and she wants to remain, this is a big hurdle to jump.

Item 5 - Each wants the other to be "an exciting sexual partner" which could be open to different interpretations. Both partners should be clear about whether their sexual needs are being met in this part of their relationship, and if not, what could be done to make sex more stimulating and enjoyable for each of them.

Item 6 - On the surface, the last item on his list support item #4 on hers. However, if you refer to item #2 on his list, you see a possible contradiction. First, he states his desire for her to be a full-time mother, but also expects her to work to help support their lifestyle. He needs to be more specific. How long does he wish her to work? Until their first child is born, or does he want her to continue working after a suitable maternity leave? There will be some discussion about the last item on her list also. It is likely he'll want to know which household chores she has in mind. No doubt it would include all of them, such as dishwashing, laundry, vacuuming, and other chores women usually do. The chapter on domestic conflicts offers some ideas for creative solutions to help decide how to divide up these jobs.

This couple would have a great deal of talking and compromising to do, on all items, before they should even consider marriage. They have disagreements in several areas, which must be resolved first. Although your expectations will no doubt vary from those given here, this exercise can be very helpful to you, because it allows you both to discuss the differences you have, and whether they can be worked out prior to marriage. Some might be considered "small stuff" and may be worked through easily. Others could be significant, which may take more time in resolving. Either way, bringing your expectations into the open could make the difference between a happy marriage or a miserable one that possibly was never meant to be in the first place.

Love

Either Partner

Am I very much in love with my partner?

In my experience, the definition of being in love varies with almost every man or woman. Many of us have heard the phrase "I love you, but I'm not in love with you." How do *you* define being in love? Is your partner the first person you think of when you're not together? Is he or she the first person you ask for advice on a given problem or situation? Do thoughts of your partner make you happy? Would you rather be with your partner than anyone else in the world? Is your partner your best friend <u>and</u> your lover? If you can answer yes to all the above, to my way of thinking, you are no doubt in love.

What if you answered no to just one question? Ask yourself why. Ideally, your partner is the person you will live with for the rest of your life. Married life has its share of frustrations as well as joys. Going through the rough patches will be a great deal easier if you know your partner and you are together because you chose each other from among all the other choices available to each of you. Of course, this applies to your partner's feelings for you too. Do you both have the same feelings for each other, or is there some disparity between you? If you find yourself with mismatched feelings, you would be well advised discussing them now.

Am I really in love or is it just a strong sexual attraction?

A relationship or marriage based solely on good sex or good looks could be heading for trouble sooner or later and it may well be sooner. It is difficult, especially in the beginning, to tell the difference between an infatuation for a person and real love. If you have known each other for a short time, sexual attraction may well be the relationship's main ingredient, which is natural after only a month or two. But if more time than that has passed, can you rationalize what other bonds are keeping you together?

Good relationships take time to develop. The amount of time spent developing a solid, nurturing relationship varies with the man and woman making up the couple. If a year or two has gone by, and you have not formed bonds other than sex, you should ask yourself whether there is basis enough to support a lifetime commitment.

Am I in love with my partner or the idea of getting married?

Do you find yourself excusing your partner's habits, attitudes or behaviors that disturb you? Is there anything in particular that you have dismissed as unimportant?

There are times when one partner is so eager to get married for his or her own reasons that he or she will ignore warning signs indicating this could be the wrong person for them. Little things seemingly insignificant now could grow into tremendous problems for either of them after marriage. Be honest with yourself about what troubles you, even if it means postponing wedding plans for an indefinite period of time.

Am I marrying too quickly after the breakup of my last long-term relationship?

We experience many emotions following the end of a relationship from which we expected more. Anger, grief, rage and denial are just four of these emotions. Sometimes, a rejected partner might be in such an emotional state that he or she isn't thinking clearly. Instead of taking the time to wade through this flood stage river of feelings, this person gets into another relationship much too soon, with either a stranger or a friend they might not have considered before. If you have gone through such an experience, can you be sure all the baggage from that prior relationship has been shipped away? How long have you been together as a couple? It couldn't hurt to give yourselves more time before taking a step as serious as exchanging your wedding vows.

Am I marrying out of love or fear of being alone?

There are times when we feel that if we don't get married now, the chance may never come our way again. The biological clock can be a powerful motivation for women who imagine time ticking away, and her best years for having children are passing her by. It can be the same for men, who want to have their families while they're young. Or it could be that you're thinking if you don't marry now, you'll end up alone, even if you don't want to have children.

Whether for a family or companionship, this type of urgency can lead to a very bad mistake if you don't take the time to know your partner and appreciate the qualities he or she has. It is far better to be lonely because you are by yourself than to be lonely because you have married someone who doesn't share at least some of your hopes and dreams.

Men's Questions

Am I marrying her because I love her, or because I'm tired of doing housework?

There is nothing wrong with wanting to have someone help out with the tasks of keeping a home, and running a house is ideally a two-person enterprise. But if love for your intended bride isn't the main reason for marriage, you would most likely be better off hiring a housekeeper than marrying one. Because a woman who discovers this fact after marriage might decide not to do housework or anything else for you in future.

Do I love her for the woman she is or something she has that I want?

The "something" could be a wealthy lifestyle, a ready-made family with one or more children, or any perceived advantage she has that you currently do not. But aside from that, is there any other common ground? Do you share any interests, be it books, music or leisure activities? Do you agree with her on most things or disagree about everything? She may have an advantage or two you've never had. She may well be a very good person, but is that "all there is?" If these are the only attractions for you, marriage would be unfair to her in the long run. Marriage here could be unfair to you as well, if you have sacrificed love only for material or emotional gain. Why not have both? It is possible, if you have the patience to wait for the right person to come along. You could achieve the financial success or other desires you have together.

Is she marrying me for love or money?

Her behavior and preferences while you are dating should be your first clues. For instance, does she only like going to places that are trendy and expensive? Has she ever suggested doing things with you that don't involve spending a lot of money?

If you have been spending a lot of money just to impress her, that could be a serious mistake. Try taking her to a less expensive, but still nice, restaurant and observe her reaction. Better yet, take her to a free concert, or for a romantic walk on the beach. Should it turn out to be a disappointment, it's better for you to know it now.

Women's Questions

Am I marrying for love or because I want a father for my current child or children?

Single parenthood is a very hard road to travel, and if you are in that situation now because you have children from a previous marriage or relationship, life may seem quite bleak at the moment. Without help financially or emotionally, marriage may be an extremely tempting prospect. Just make sure that you love and care for the man himself, not because he simply represents a meal ticket and instant child care assistance. Be certain that he not only loves your children but you as well.

Make it a point to spend time together as a family, and try to arrange evenings alone as a couple, so you will have a better idea if the two of you are well-matched or not. Find out what your likes and dislikes are, and how many interests you have in common that you can build on together. You may not think it is important, but these things do matter after a while.

Am I marrying him for love or only for financial and emotional security?

If your reasons for marriage have more to do with financial security and less with love and caring for him, you may be on very shaky ground. If he happened to suffer a financial reverse, where would that leave you? Put quite simply; poor, unhappy and stuck in an emotionally barren marriage. Is that what you really want? Assuming he is a good, decent person who really loves you, he deserves better than that.

Susan S. Levine

Is he marrying me for love or because I'm pregnant?

Getting pregnant intentionally to push a man into commitment is a gamble which may or may not get you the result you want. He could choose to walk away entirely. Or he could decide to "do the right thing" and agree to marriage for the sake of the child on the way. But this is not the best way to begin a marriage. Had he shown *any* interest in marriage before your pregnancy? If not, it is unlikely that taking away his freedom of choice would make him happy about the idea. That may not have been what you intended, but that is still what you have done.

Do you really feel a marriage of obligation, if that's all it is, is fair, to him or your unborn child? Children do not ask to be born. But if they could ask, don't you think they would want two parents who will love them and give them a happy home? My guess is that they would. Think long and hard, if you are getting married for this reason alone. More couples should realize "Babies don't make marriages!"

Sex

Either Partner

Does my partner find sex unpleasant?

If your partner seems turned off by sex in any way, this is an issue that must be discussed immediately. It cannot and should not be avoided, hoping it will go away. Try to find reasons for this aversion to sex. There could be just one, possibly several. Needless to say, it is an extremely sensitive topic, and may be very difficult for your partner to talk about. Your sympathy and understanding will be very important.

However, you should be prepared for your partner's refusal to discuss the matter or get help in a professional capacity. And if that occurs, that leaves you in a very tough spot. You obviously can't *force* someone to seek help. But then you must consider whether marriage would be wise at this time.

Does my partner ask what I like and what feels good to me?

Everyone has their own ideas on what makes a partner a good lover. Does consideration for your sexual needs and desires rate high on your partner's list? It should. Of course, that should apply to you as well. If your partner seems uncomfortable with a certain act or position, it might be a good idea to ask what he or she would prefer. And if there is anything you are hesitant or unwilling to do, you should not feel afraid or nervous about saying "No."

Do my partner and I have matching sex drives?

Assuming you have been involved in a sexual relationship with your partner, are you both on the same level of desire you had in the beginning? Sometimes one partner will develop an increased sex drive, while the other partner's appears to decline. Has this occurred in your relationship? If so, is there a specific reason? Declining sexual interest has more than one cause. It could be physical or emotional or even medical, but you should discuss the problem and do what you can to find out what its source is. Entering into marriage with this type of unresolved conflict can lead to trouble sooner or later. While it is true that good sex is not the only basis for a happy and fulfilling marriage, it is still a very important one, and must not be ignored.

Men's Questions

Am I content with the sexual part of our relationship?

There can be many reasons why women are not in the mood at the same time you might be. If your intended spouse seems to finding too many reasons for not wanting sex, you obviously have a problem. The source of the difficulty could be almost anything, but it is up to you to ask, in a non-confrontational way, what you could do to help. You may find it is a situation outside your relationship that is troubling her, and all she needs to do is talk about it. But you'll never know if you don't take the time to find out.

Do I feel comfortable with my partner initiating sex?

Although many men are happy when their girlfriends or wives make sexual overtures to them, others may feel resentful and refuse. What are *your* feelings about it? Have you ever turned down your partner's request for sex simply because it wasn't your idea? And does it really matter to you whose idea it is, as long as you're both enjoying a satisfying sexual relationship? If it does matter, do some serious self-examination and find out why.

Women's Questions

Do I enjoy sex as a healthy, normal and loving part of our relationship?

Most women can respond with an enthusiastic yes! However, you might be in the minority of women that consider sex an unpleasant duty, not an enjoyable activity. Have you asked yourself why this is the case? Could it be physical or emotional? Is it based upon the way you were raised? Feelings about sex instilled by our parents can be difficult to overcome. Only you can answer this question.

Whatever the cause, the needs of your prospective husband must also be considered. If he is a healthy man with an active sex drive, you can hardly expect him to be content with infrequent–and very likely grudging–sex for the rest of his life. Has he expressed concern about your lack of desire, and if he has, what was your response? If you really love him and your relationship is good in every other way, seek help. Talking to an objective third party, such as a sex therapist, psychologist, or other professional, is a step you should seriously consider *before* taking the walk down the aisle.

What acts of lovemaking does he like that I do not?

This would depend on what they are. Oral sex, performed by you or by him, is sometimes an issue for women, and they are not comfortable with it, even though it's enjoyed by other couples. This is only one example, and it may not apply in your case. But whatever it is you have a problem with, it should be discussed, even though it may not be easy for either of you to talk about.

Susan S. Levine

"A woman has got to love a bad man once or twice in her life to be thankful for a good one."

(Mae West, 1892-1980)

Personal Characteristics

Either Partner

Am I a team player or more of a loner?

Being a good team player means working as part of a group, not just for yourself. In marriage, that team is just two people, you and your partner. Loners are more accustomed to working by themselves. While there isn't anything necessarily wrong with working on your own, problems can and do arise in marriage where the loner has a habit of acting as if there isn't another person involved.

Talking with your partner can bring these differences in personality out into the open, where agreements could be worked out.

Do I or my partner have a need to be "right?"

Before you answer, think carefully. When you get into arguments–or heated discussions–do either of you have a habit of saying "am I right" feeling sure that you are? Knowing you are right can make *you* feel good, but there is bound to be some resentment from your partner. Remember that you are now in a relationship with a very special person. Consistently being "right" may have served you well as captain of a debating team, but will undoubtedly cause stress and unhappiness to someone who is continually, by default, put in the wrong by you.

Being in a relationship requires compromise, and the willingness to see the differences in your partner positively. If you or your partner can't let go of the need to be right about everything, your marriage may begin to resemble a battlefield, with each of you striving to outdo the other. Why not try to make a few changes now? Just ask yourself (or your partner), when you find yourselves struggling with the right-wrong issue, how important it really is at the time. In working through a difficult situation, it is important to negotiate a solution that works for the benefit of both partners, not to gratify just the ego of one. If you can start putting this goal into practice, you may find yourself believing that being right all the time isn't as important as you thought.

Do we have the same outlooks on life?

Would you choose a business partner who had a negative view of any new idea or product you proposed? Not likely. Who wants to hear ideas shot down as soon as we think them up? Having a life partner who shares our positive view of things can make a big difference in a marriage. Imagine what life would be like with a partner who gave you *little or no* encouragement, whether it was when going for a new job, while you were developing a new interest, or learning a new skill. It would probably become very depressing to you in a very short period of time.How do you find out if your partner has a positive or negative outlook on life in general? By talking about your views and ideas and observing your partner's reaction. If he or she seems negative on everything, ask why. It could be due to just having a bad day. However, if this negative attitude persists no matter what topic you are discussing, and into every day, you may want to ask yourself if marriage to this person would be the right decision for you.

Could my partner help me through a personal crisis?

Have you experienced an emotional upheaval while in this relationship? A death of a close relative or friend? A career setback or loss of a job? If so, how did your partner behave toward you? What assistance did he or she offer? Sometimes a sympathetic ear and a shoulder to cry on are all we need. Some partners are not sure what to do, so they do nothing. Or worse yet, there are those who will become unavailable because they don't want to deal with your pain.

Is your partner someone you can rely on during the bad times as well as the good ones? If your answer is no, marriage to this person could be a serious mistake. However, if you're just not sure, because you haven't suffered bad experiences in your relationship yet, it is probably too early to make a final judgement. But it might be wise to delay marriage until you have your answer.

Are we able to say no without feeling guilty?

Most of us want to be able to help out friends and relatives when they need it. But this desire to assist them can go too far if you don't know how to say "no" on some occasions. There are people who are so fearful of having anyone angry with them for refusing a request, that they go overboard and try to accommodate everyone. Do you or your partner fall into this category? If so, all you may need is a little self-training. When someone asks you to do them a favor and it's simply impossible for you to oblige them at that moment, just tell the person you can't, at this time.

It is important to begin this training now. Developing an ability to say "no" can be essential in a marriage. For example, would you want to be carrying out favors for friends right after you're married? Remember, it is supposed to be your special time, for you and your partner to be spending as newlyweds. If the person you refuse accuses you of being selfish, don't take it personally. Does this mean you should never do favors for others? Of course not! You just need to be more selective of the favors you do. Your friends or family will probably be annoyed at first, but that's not a big deal. And if you are consistent with your refusal of demands you feel are unreasonable, eventually they will stop asking.

Money

Either Partner

What are my feelings about money?

Although the issue of money may not seem so important right now, it has the potential to cause a great deal of problems if you do not make it a point to discuss how you each handle money. How do you feel about money in general? Do you believe it's impolite to talk about it? Do you feel that the way you manage money is no one else's business? How much do you know about the value of money? Money is never an easy subject to talk about, but when you are thinking of marriage to anyone, it cannot and should not be ignored. Arguments over money cause more couples to arrive in divorce court than almost any other topic.

If you're not sure what questions you should ask your partner about money, get down to your bookstore or library and get yourself one or two books on the subject. One excellent source of information is Suze Orman's book, <u>The Courage To Be Rich</u>, specifically to the "Love and Money" section. She provides a great deal of detail on what money matters you should be aware of when contemplating marriage, and the type of red flags you or your partner may be waving.

How does my partner handle credit?

It's hard to determine this if you're not already living together, but if you go over to your partner's house and see a stack of unpaid bills on the table, that's a definite clue. Ideally, bills should be paid as soon as they come in, but many prefer to wait until close to the due date, especially if they're waiting for a paycheck to deposit into their account first. Obviously, you can't mail a check to the utility company if there is not enough money in the account to cover it.

However, the issue of credit is a very serious one, since it affects everything you want to do in the future, such as buying a house, financing a continuing education, or anything else requiring a strong credit rating. If you or your partner have not been paying close attention to each other's bill payments track record, start now, before it comes back to haunt you later. It is never too soon to strengthen your credit record, since you never know when a good credit history will come in handy.

Can my partner be too tight-fisted?

We have all heard the saying "penny-wise but pound-foolish." Are you or your partner the type of person who will drive out of the way to spend one or two less dollars on sale items? There are times when comparison shopping is a virtue or a fault, depending on what the product is. Couples and families who need to be very careful about spending money unnecessarily due to a limited income are not being miserly, just cautious, and justly so. However, if one of you makes a good living, enough to support a comfortable lifestyle, if not extravagant, but is unwilling to spend money for the smallest luxuries, married life with this person could be very difficult over time.

Does my partner invest money in high-risk ventures?

That would depend on whether or not your partner believes in having separate accounts. It would be wise to establish a rule that no household money should be used for this purpose, since high-risk investments have a very good chance of going downhill with little or no warning. Otherwise, they wouldn't be called "high risk!"

Does my partner overspend on perceived "necessities?"

It is very important to spot this tendency now, because these so-called necessities could be big-ticket items like flashy cars, boats (which have a continual incoming tide of expenses just for maintenance alone), or new homes that might cost far more than your combined incomes could pay the monthly mortgage on. The list can go on and on and the cost of these "toys"–plus the maintenance–can wipe out combined savings, ruin credit ratings, and could ultimately lead to bankruptcy both financially and in your relationship as well. Does your partner have extras he/she could easily do without? Ask direct questions of your partner, BEFORE you get married, how he/she paid for the luxuries, and whether they are actually paid for in full, or is your partner in hock to the bank or credit card companies?

Your partner's reaction will be either to display great discomfort and refuse giving you an honest answer or they will simply become angry while insisting it is none of your business. If you're not married, the latter comment is correct...for now. But the moment you get married, what your partner does as an individual will also affect you, your partner, and ultimately your children if you decide to have them.

If you find your partner's excessive spending unacceptable, make that clear immediately. Some people are simply compulsive spenders, and obtaining counseling for this problem could be a step in the right direction for you both. You should insist that this must be done before getting married.

Men's Questions

Am I willing for us to have two individual accounts and one joint account?

This would mean a little extra work for you, but this option allows you both to have your own money to spend for personal needs. For example, she might enjoy playing tennis and you don't. You might have a taste for more expensive designer clothes, but she usually buys clothes at discount stores. Having your own accounts, in addition to the joint account for household expenses, gives you both the freedom to indulge your personal desires without arguing over who spends too much on what. As long as each of you deposits a percentage of your paycheck into your own account and your joint household expense account, it can make life easier in many ways. The percentages would vary according the amount of your incomes. Add up the monthly household expenses to see how much must be deposited by each of you to maintain the joint account to pay those bills. Then see how much is left over, to determine your combined discretionary income. Split that amount in half, and figure out how much can go into your individual accounts weekly, every two weeks, or each month, depending on how often you are paid.

Women's Questions

Do I want to put all of my paycheck into one joint account?

It may be easier to deposit all of your paycheck into one joint account, but does that mean it's the best move for you? Assuming you have your own checking account now, there would really be no reason to close it just because you get married. What about personal expenses, such as clothes, shoes, cosmetics, and the other items women purchase regularly? You don't want to be put in the position of having to justify every personal expense you make to your spouse.

How would your partner feel about it? Make sure you talk about separate accounts with him and find out. Most men shouldn't have a problem with your having an account of your own, but what if he does? Find out why, before you get married. If you are both working and have no children, why should you not have money of your own?

If you are in charge of your own account, then you are also responsible for maintaining the records of deposits and withdrawals, so this individual account would not cause him inconvenience. But if he is still uncomfortable with this idea, even after you have presented your reasons why this should be done, ask yourself what his reasons could be. Why is he turning such a small matter into such a big deal? Although you should be contributing the higher percentage of your weekly or monthly paycheck into a joint account to pay for monthly household expenses, you should also have money to pay for things you want, without having to ask his permission.

Suggest that you each have your own accounts, and a third one for joint expenses. You both can decide how much of your paychecks can go into your private accounts and how much can go into the joint account. The joint account should have enough in it every month to cover your costs for housing, transportation, food, utility bills, and all other expenses necessary to maintain your home. When you add those up, you'll have a better idea of how much you can put into your individual accounts.

"Age does not protect you from love, but love to some extent protects you from age."

(Jeanne Moreau)

Family

Either Partner

How do I feel about parenthood?

No matter how small or big they are, children present a tremendous challenge. When they are infants, new parents have to cope with the 24-hour, seven-day job of dealing with feedings, sometimes near constant crying while they're teething or ill and messy diapers, to name just some of the little inconveniences children bring into your marriage with them. Then comes the toddler stage, the terrible twos, and it goes on until they become young adults and each age group has its own set of peculiarities and problems challenging both parents.

If you are at all unsure of how you will be able to handle the responsibility of parenthood, the time to speak is NOW. Not after you're married, and certainly not after you (if you're female) or your partner (if you're male) becomes pregnant. What happens if you do not want children but your partner does? Or if the opposite is the case? You have an issue that must be discussed and resolved, one way or another, before marriage can be considered.

Would a child bring joy or stress to our marriage?

Even to a couple that is prepared to accept the roles of mom and dad, children bring healthy amounts of each. If you are the mother, you have to decide whether to be a stay-home or working mom. As a father, you may have to work more hours to support three people on one income, if your partner stops working. Of course, your circumstances may be different. But one fact remains: you would now have a new little person who must be cared for.

Have you had a pretty easy lifestyle so far? With both you and your partner working and bringing in two incomes, you were free to do whatever you wanted, as long as you had the money to do so. Once your baby is born, those carefree times will be a thing of the past for some time to come, unless you have family or friends who can be relied on for baby sitting.

If there is no one helping you out with the day-to-day tasks of caring for a new baby, it could be a very long time before you have anything but highly limited time for yourselves. You might say there is always the time when the baby sleeps. But some couples have babies who are either very light sleepers, or seem to manage with almost no sleep at all. What would you do then?

Some people have higher stress tolerance levels than others and can handle the challenges of child care more easily. For new moms or dads with low levels of stress tolerance, a few nights with a colicky, screaming infant may be more than they can deal with. Find out what your saturation stress level is before deciding on whether you want to take on the job of raising a family.

How would we react to something going wrong?

Although we hope that our children will be happy and healthy, sadly there are times when parents strike out on both counts, due to a serious physical or mental illness diagnosed after birth, or in early childhood. Have you considered the effect such an event could have on you as a couple? If you are parents with limited financial resources and little or no insurance, the effect can be devastating. In addition to the emotional heartbreak suffered, you would also find yourselves having to pay some staggering medical costs. This is the type of potential disaster which over time could wipe out whatever savings you have.

If you are prepared, financially and emotionally, to cope with the possibility–which always exists–of raising and caring for a handicapped child, go for it. If not, it would wise to postpone having children.

Have we talked about the size of our future family?

You both have agreed that you want to raise a family, but have you jointly decided how many children you should have? It would be wise to consider the sizes of your combined incomes before you commit yourselves to having a large family, which usually includes more than two children. You may have always dreamed of having a big family, with maybe four children, especially if you have happy memories of your family as you grew up. But remember one important fact: your parents paid *all* the bills. This time, the financial pressures will be on your shoulders. And if you or your partner becomes a stay-at-home mom, money can well become an even bigger issue than it may have been in the pre-family rearing portion of your marriage.

It's not only finances that must be considered when deciding how many children you want to have. Realistically, your ages matter as well. If you are both young, in your early, middle or late twenties, you probably have higher energy levels. What if you're both in your early to middle thirties? Would you be willing, not to mention able, to chase after energetic kids when you both are in your late thirties or early forties? As the mother of a nine-year-old boy, I can honestly say that it takes a lot of energy to keep up with him. He was born when I was 35. You may think now that age doesn't make a difference, but that will probably change as you grow older. Keeping in mind the reality of how much money, time and energy you have to spend can help you make the best decision, for you and the children in your future.

Men's Questions

Do I want to be a father?

While some men have always wanted to be dads and raise a family of their own, there is no rule written stating you must become a father after you are married. If you are in your early twenties, you might not be ready for such a responsibility right now. You might be older than that, and have decided that fatherhood is not right for you at any time in your life. There is nothing wrong with that. Every man is different, and no one should feel pressured to have a child, whether the pressure comes from well-meaning parents, in-laws, or other relatives and friends.

If you feel you are not ready for the challenges being a father poses, make sure you tell your future wife–or any women you choose to date–how you feel. If they want children but you do not, it is best that they know this as soon as you feel it is appropriate to tell them. The earlier, the better, since you shouldn't waste their time or yours. This knowledge shared between you obviously means birth control should be a primary consideration in any sexual relationship that might develop between you.

How do I feel about taking care of a baby?

Many new dads are not only willing but eager to assist their wives with these jobs, and will help whenever they can. Other men refer to these chores as "women's work" and refuse to offer any assistance. If you grew up in a household where your mom did all the housework, cooking and child care and your dad worked at an outside job, you probably think this is perfectly natural. Which it may be...for you.

Your future wife may have been raised within a completely different environment, where both parents were active care givers for herself and her siblings if she has any. Contrary to what you may prefer to believe, what was good for your mother is not necessarily good for your wife. Assuming you have had any discussions on this topic, you may see by now that she has opposing views from yours on this matter. The question is whether or not a compromise can be reached.

Women's Questions

Do I want to be a mother?

Whether you want to be a mother or not is a decision that can and should only be made by YOU. If you are very young, you may feel that you are not ready for such a responsibility for a few years. There is nothing wrong with that at all, and you should not feel you're being selfish for making this decision. Whatever your age may be, do not let anyone, be it your fiancé, your parents, your prospective in-laws or your friends pressure you into believing otherwise.

Once children are born, you cannot return them just because you were not ready for the tremendous amount of work they present. They must be fed, changed, entertained, loved, and they may not always spend their time sleeping. You may have to go for more than a few nights without sleep, especially if your baby develops colic and can cry for hours at a time. Make sure you are completely ready to take on the challenges of motherhood, physically and emotionally, before you even consider becoming pregnant.

Am I ready to give up my career?

Although some jobs today offer perks like flexible hours and job sharing, there are some career choices requiring you to stay on a less flexible and more particular path, if you hope to reach the top in your profession. Let us assume, as an example, that you are an attorney. If you have been working at a law firm, the top is usually a partnership. So the question for you is how much going off a well defined path leading to a partnership for a time will cost you in terms of achieving your goal. Your priorities may have changed from the time you first became a member of the firm you are working for, and the goal of partner doesn't seem as important as it used to be. If that is the case, motherhood may take you off the career path for a few years, but if you are willing to assume a less demanding position, if and when you decide to return to the legal world, you may be able to find a job allowing you to more evenly balance work and family.

However, if the goal of being a full partner is still very important to you, it may be considerably more than just "difficult" to balance the demands of motherhood and career. Something is going to be neglected, despite your best efforts, particularly if your husband also has a demanding job, and cannot take much time off to assist with a new family member. Of course, you can always hire someone if you both make a high salary. But then someone else is getting all the benefits of being close to your child, not you. Someone else is leaving "their" impression on "your" child instead of yours and your spouse's. And with both parents working long hours, your child will not have either of you to play and interact with.

Give the idea of motherhood a great deal of thought, and discuss it at length with your partner before deciding to get married. If he thinks you should be the one to give up your career simply because you are a woman, marriage with him might not be in your best interests.

Career

Either Partner

Do we enjoy talking about our careers?

Since most of us don't quit our jobs after we get married, our work remains very important, unless you hate your job. What is your reaction to your partner's job, and vice versa? Do you feel it's not important or less than interesting? Do you or your partner make unfavorable remarks about your respective jobs?

Maybe it doesn't matter right now. But what about later? If you're one of the lucky people who really love what they do, it could be a big disappointment not to be able to talk about it with your partner. If your partner doesn't like to hear about your job, for example, ask why. There are a number of reasons for this, such as insecurity, jealousy or envy. If you (as a female reader) are making more money than your spouse, this too can become a cause for concern and may damage a delicate male ego.

If these emotions sound like the same thing, they aren't. Feelings of insecurity could make your partner feel the job is more exciting than he or she is. Your partner may be jealous–for whatever reason–of the time you spend on the job. Or envious of the fact that you have a job you love while your partner doesn't. These and other reasons could all be possible causes for hostility towards your job. Sometimes a little reassurance to your partner can make a big difference. Or it may not. But it will be a source of trouble eventually if one or both of you feels uncomfortable talking about your careers.

Am I happy with my partner's career choice?

Professions such as medicine, law, law enforcement, nursing, firefighting and the military *(to name just a few!)* all have very demanding hours of work; these are not your typical nine-to-five positions. A person just entering any of these fields will be away from home a good deal, which can be very hard on a new marriage. If you believe you cannot accept the demands of your partner's career without complaining about their time spent away from home, or making him or her feel guilty because of it, you have two options. Either postpone marriage for a year or two until your partner is more settled in that career, or end the relationship now, and find a partner whose work schedule is easier to deal with. Forcing a partner to decide between his or her career and you is a gamble you are almost certain to lose.

Would I be willing to move if my partner got a new job?

Whether you could find a situation comparable to your present one in another city which offers the same salary and benefits depends on the job you have now. Some positions can be found almost anywhere, such as administrative assistant, or computer programmer; while others that might be considered "executive" jobs are more difficult to obtain in another city. Moving is never easy, and if you do not feel you can make the transition; giving up your family and friends, for a city, town or even country that could be very difficult to live in, marriage might be have to be postponed for the time being.

Do I consider my career more important than my partner's?

A higher salary is important economically, but it does not make your partner's career less valuable because of a lower compensation level. It wouldn't be very wise or tactful to tell your partner that since you make the larger income, your needs must always come first. If you honestly believe that the "bigger bucks speak louder," you are not going to be a giving partner in a marriage. Marriage often requires compromise, and this means you will not always get your own way. If this does not agree with you, it is better not to get married right now.

Men's Questions

If my job requires frequent travel, will she understand?

What has her attitude toward your job been like so far? Has she complained about missed dates, or not having enough time with you? Does she become annoyed at times when a sudden trip for business reasons interrupts plans made in advance? You may have to decide whether the demands of your job are worth the time spent away from your partner. If your career is important to you, you should discuss it with her before getting married, especially if the job requires traveling for an indefinite period of time.

Women's Questions

As a military wife, how would I feel about moving every few years?

Military couples without children can move around more easily than military families. Very often, families can find it very difficult to obtain housing outside the base if on-base housing is unavailable. And depending on the surrounding area, the cost of apartments or rental homes can be very high. If he/she is ordered to transfer to a foreign country for a year or more, there is the problem of learning a new language and living within a culture that may be too different for you to accept.

Consider all these scenarios very carefully. You can get quite a few perks from being a military wife, but the prospect of a frequently-absent husband may not be the vision of married life you had in mind. If that is the case, speak up now, because once you're married, it is too late. If you're concerned about being a military wife, you should become aware of the excellent support groups offered to military wives to help them through long periods of loneliness while he's away from home.

Susan S. Levine

"Everyone admits that love is wonderful and necessary, yet no one agrees on just what it is."

(Diane Ackerman)

Health

Either Partner

Are we both in good physical health?

Now is a good time to find this out, because if one partner has a serious illness, it could be a large factor in your decision to marry. Would you still marry if one of you is HIV positive?

(If the answer is no for one partner) Would a serious illness have a negative impact on our marriage?

If the illness is considered terminal, like cancer or leukemia, to name just two, it will definitely have an impact, and a good deal of it will be negative. Illnesses like this affect a patient's physical and emotional state, and he or she will need a strong and loving partner for support, companionship and love. It will be very hard, and the healthy partner must know if he or she is strong enough to meet this challenge.

Would we stand by each other if one of us becomes seriously ill?

One of the traditional marriage vows demands remaining together "...in sickness and in health," but very often the reality of a severe illness is more than a partner is prepared for. You both need to discuss this at length, and if one of you expresses an active dislike of "nurse duties," it is better to know this before marriage. Most of us would want a concerned, caring partner around us if we become very sick, rather than someone who regards it as a disagreeable inconvenience. After all, nobody asks to be ill, and when they are, it's not their fault.

Are either of us repulsed by the effects of a serious illness or accident?

Again, you both need to do a great deal of self-examination to arrive at the answer to this question. Whether by illness or accident, if it is severe enough, the body can sustain terrible damage in all areas; physical disfigurement and full or partial paralysis are only two aspects of what your partner could suffer. It is possible that the brain could also be affected, leaving the patient in a vegetative, comatose state, or in milder cases, leave speech, other important bodily or mobile functions noticeably damaged.

None of us really knows how they will react to such a situation. We all like to believe we'd be strong for our partner and stand by to take care of our loved one, no matter what it took. However, if you believe otherwise, that you would probably bolt at the first sign of difficulty, you have to ask yourself whether you are mature enough to handle such a responsibility, should the worst happen.

How does my partner react when I'm not well?

A simple bug like a head cold is a big deal when we're the ones suffering from it. And when we're wiped out by this nasty little virus, we usually expect a little sympathy from our partners, even if we don't require round-the-clock nursing care. What has been your partner's attitude while you were ill in the past? Was he or she concerned about your welfare? Has she/he asked you if you wanted some company? Would they have driven over to your house with chicken soup even when you didn't ask? The way your partner treats you when you have a minor illness can often be indicative of their future reaction to a more serious or even life-threatening one.

Of course, if you want your partner's sympathy and support when you are ill, you should be prepared to go the extra mile or two for your partner when the occasion arises. Maybe he or she wouldn't want your help. Some people just want to be alone when they're sick. But it shouldn't hurt your relationship if you make it a priority to offer aid and comfort when necessary. At the very least your partner will know you truly care for them.

Is there serious mental or physical illness in either of our families?

Couples planning to have children should make it a priority to ask their parents and other relatives about severe illnesses in their families. Even though each partner is healthy, any children they have could be afflicted with a mental or physical disability. It is much better to know whether such conditions exist before marriage.

If one or both families are affected, it doesn't mean you shouldn't marry. But it could increase the possibility that one or all of your children, if you decide to have them, might be diagnosed with a medical problem shortly after birth or in early childhood. You should think very carefully before deciding to take that chance. It's a very wise practice to compare family medical histories before marriage and certainly to have full information available to both partners after marrying and prior to deciding upon getting pregnant.

Faith

Either Partner

Does religion make a difference to our relationship?

If you both share the same faith, probably not. Religion usually becomes an issue when two partners come from two different belief systems, and each has a strong attachment to his and her own faith. Since the customs and beliefs of some religions can vary a great deal, it can cause problems when the partners decide to marry.

How would I feel about converting, if asked?

It would depend on how strong your religious feelings are, and the degree of attachment to your own faith. When my parents married, my father was required to take Catholic instruction and agree to raise any children in the marriage's future as Catholics. His background was Protestant, but he was never a churchgoer, so this condition was not a problem for him.

But let's say that the male partner is Jewish and the female partner a Christian. If he insists that his future wife must convert to Judaism as a marriage condition, she would have to give up the customs she grew up with, especially the Christmas and Easter holidays. She must decide how important they are to her, and whether she really wants to give them up. Marriage should not be considered until her decision is made.

Do I expect my partner to convert?

Some religious institutions will not even consider doing interfaith marriages, so the question of conversion will likely come up before any ceremony takes place. If you want a formal church wedding, and your priest or minister won't compromise on this issue, you have to discuss this with your partner. If neither of you have strong religious feelings, and you want to get married, you can do this with a civil ceremony. By choosing the second option, you keep the question of religion out, and the process of getting married may become much simpler.

Additionally, if either you or your partner are divorced, you may well find the only easy method of legally tying the knot is to simply avail yourselves of the services of either a Notary Public or city or county official licensed by your state to perform marriages. Many religions will simply NOT marry a couple when either or both of them have been divorced. Some religions actually do not consider a dissolution of marriage by divorce decree as carrying more weight than your original marriage vows taken under the auspices of their religious belief system.

Politics

Either Partner

How would we handle opposing views?

That really depends on the type of people you are. Have you ever had discussions on various political issues, and if so, did you have them for the sake of debate, or did you find them becoming much too personal? You must decide what is most important to you, and whether you prefer your partner to share most, if not all, of the beliefs you have on certain issues. If true love can win over politics, it shouldn't matter at all.

Do we discuss or argue about our differences?

Conservatives and liberals often clash on various issues, but if you are in a relationship with a partner whose views you actively dislike, I don't see how you're not going to take a political discussion personally. Neither of you are probably going to change your ideologies to suit the other, so you must decide, when you talk about politics, that you aren't going to take your partner's opposition to your views as a personal attack. The same applies to your partner. Otherwise, you are going to have a lot of arguments that may be difficult to patch up later.

Susan S. Levine

"In matrimony, to hesitate is sometimes to be saved."

(Samuel Butler)

Common Interests

Either Partner

What leisure activities do we both like?

Many couples could have different activities that the other partner doesn't share, but it helps if you can share and be passionate about just one. It could be anything, whether gardening, fixing up a home, or community involvement in a particular area. Explore all possibilities, and don't give up until you find something you want to share as a couple.

Does my partner encourage me to pursue my interests?

Just because your partner doesn't share your taste for the same types of books, TV programs, movies, or music you like does not mean they are without value to you. If your partner seems to be making unwelcome or unkind comments about your particular tastes however, it could be a source of potential serious conflict later on. You might try talking with your partner about why your interests seem to make him or her uncomfortable. But don't think you should give up your interests simply to suit your partner.

Would my partner try something new?

That might depend on whether the new interest is similar to the one your partner enjoys. For example, you both might like Police Procedural programs, but one of you watches "Law and Order" while the other watches "NYPD Blue." I had a similar situation a few years ago, when my husband would watch the Arts and Entertainment Sherlock Holmes series with me, but refused to consider "Law and Order," during which I was glued to the set for an hour on Wednesday evenings. Since I knew he would like it if he tried watching it, I began taping the earlier "Law and Order" programs aired on A&E to keep around in case we had what we called a "dead TV" night.

The next time one of those nights came around, I popped in one of the videocassettes, not telling my husband what it was at first. By the time the program ended, he asked if there were any more on the tape. Sometimes, you do have to resort to one or two tricks. But if it results in sharing a new interest you didn't have before, a little "trickery" isn't so bad.

Little Domestic Conflicts

It's amazing how so-called "little" disagreements can escalate into large battles after a time of living with conflicting domestic ideas. Knowing ahead of time what your partner's likes and dislikes are can pave the way for dealing with situations as they arise, and finding a way to work around them.

Either Partner

Are our body temperatures the same?

Very often we find that our partners are the polar opposites of ourselves, and in the most literal sense. You may prefer the cooler weather of the Fall, Winter and early Spring seasons, while your partner lives for the summer...with as little air conditioning as possible.

That may not be an issue now, but when you begin living together as a married couple, that will change very quickly. You may find that all the windows you have *opened* to air out the house or apartment on a cool, breezy day have been *closed* a little while later because for your spouse it was too cold. The heating bills will probably rise during the winter, but so will the electric bills during the summer, if you favor more air conditioning. And you may find that if you have central air conditioning, the thermometer will be changed quite frequently. You will have to be very creative and discuss ways you can work around this very basic problem so it's not a running battle.

Do we have opposite sleeping schedules?

If one of you has to be up very early in the morning for work, but the other doesn't, you may have a sleeping conflict to work out, especially if you or your partner likes to stay up until the wee hours of the morning. Sometimes a partner who has to be in bed early to get enough rest for the next day might resent the fact their partner doesn't want to sleep at the same time as he or she does. But there one or two things you can do to keep arguments from developing. The partner who is a night owl could agree to an early night one or two evenings a week. If sleep doesn't come during that time, there are other ways to relax.

Do we resemble Felix and Oscar?

Felix and Oscar, for those who are not baby boomers, were the two characters in an early 1960's sitcom, "The Odd Couple." This was a continuation of the stage play written by Neil Simon. In this comedy, Felix was the personification of the word "neatnik," while Oscar was, well, the more *casual* of the two. Okay, I'll say it, Oscar was a *slob*. You may find that you and your partner resemble these characters in terms of living style. And, if that's the case, then it is almost a sure thing you will find yourselves arguing about it more than once. The question is, how often?

This is one issue that should be seriously considered, because while Felix or Oscar could walk out if they felt like it, you won't have that option. If *you know* exactly where your dirty clothes go, but *your partner* doesn't seem to have a clue, then you'll certainly need to make a joint decision about that. Once you've both decided on the place for putting them (a hamper next to the washer/dryer, or in the closet is the ideal choice---*she said* assertively) and stick with your decision. No doubt some other creative solutions will be necessary. But if you work them out together, without arguments or insults, they could even be fun.

Who Should Do What?

You could go with the traditional model, where the woman does "female stuff," like cooking, laundry, grocery shopping, vacuuming and other cleaning, and the man does all car-related work, lawn care, and household repairs. But what if you, as a female reader, hate to cook, but love tinkering with the family car? What if you, as a male reader, hate doing handywork, but enjoy going grocery shopping? The solution in both cases is easy; you just decide who *likes* doing certain things, and who doesn't. You can also decide which things you "both" like and perhaps gain some extra "together" time doing them that way!

Sometimes it isn't that simple. Who knows anyone who actually *enjoys* taking out the garbage, cleaning the bathroom, or vacuuming the floors? But these tasks still have to be done eventually, and if you're not wealthy enough to hire a full-time cleaning crew, you may have to take turns with the jobs you love to hate.

It may not be so disagreeable for either of you, if you agree to take on equally distasteful tasks at the same time. That way, you don't get into an argument about how you spent the whole afternoon cleaning the bathroom while your partner relaxed and read a book. Coming up with imaginative solutions to cleaning conflicts could get the jobs done a lot faster. Then you might reward yourselves with a nice romantic evening out.

What are the things that drive me nuts?

By now, if you've known each other long, some quirks may be showing themselves. But they probably won't concern you much until you begin living together in the same place. Giving a list of what drives men and women crazy might help, but since every man and woman is different, it might be better to make your own lists. And actually, this too could be fun. There's really no reason all of this can't be looked upon as a "fun activity," provided both partners are serious about completing these personal assessments as a method of closer bonding and for future mutual happiness.

When I was in high school, I played on a girls field hockey team. And at every game we played with another school, the prayer was always the same:

> **"God grant me the serenity to accept the things I cannot change, the courage to change the things I can, and the wisdom to know the difference."**

Why the coach chose that particular prayer remains a mystery to me, since we seldom won a game, but constant repetition over four years made it stick. But if you think about it, that same prayer could be applied very well in a marriage. Particularly on the domestic front.

There are some things about your mate that drive you crazy, but cannot be changed. Those are the personality quirks, like putting the knives or forks in the dish rack with the points up. You *know* they should go points downward! Constant reminders won't help, trust me on this one. You'll end up turning them over yourself. Other little things might have the same effect, but these can be changed. Those are simply bad habits, like your mate dropping clothes wherever he or she happens to be. The clothing hamper might help there, and maybe your mate could choose the location, even if it seems *bizarre* to you (after all, "you" know it belongs by the washer/dryer!). You could always hide it if company suddenly shows up.

But let's go back to the list. If your mate does not want to participate in these personal and interpersonal assessments, pressure won't help. Just do one for yourself. Get a nice sheet of paper–the larger the better–and write at

Susan S. Levine

the top: "Grant Me:" and then go down and make two
columns. The first heading should be "Serenity to Accept."
In that column, write down all the little things about your
mate that you know you *can't* change, even if they make
you want to explode at times. The second column should
be headed, "Courage to Change." List here everything that
you find annoying, but you feel *can* be changed, even if it
could take months. If you're still puzzled over how your
form should look, the visual aid provided below may help.

Grant Me:
Serenity to Accept   Courage to Change

Ask Me About Wisdom Tomorrow

Your lists in each column can be short or long, it is up
to you. If you have a talent for crafts, you could make your
lists into a nice table or wall plaque using calligraphy or
other artistic lettering, show it to your friends, and start a
little craft business. Of course, this is just an idea, and you
certainly don't have to do it. But it can be a fun way to
lighten the mood when you may be having an off day.

Remember that this exercise is purely for fun, and isn't
meant to address the more serious issues that may come up
after marriage. But it could help keep you from dwelling

on the small stuff, especially if you can find the ability to laugh about it.

"Life is to be fortified by many friendships. To love and be loved is the greatest happiness of existence."

(Sydney Smith)

Personal Behaviors And Habits

Either Partner

Does my partner abuse alcohol or drugs?

If he or she does, it's obvious something is terribly wrong. Alcohol and drugs *do* alter the abuser's behavior, despite their protests to the contrary. The behavioral changes can range from emotional and physical withdrawal from their family and friends to episodes of violent temper, which may not even be remembered when the effects of the substance have worn off.

Do you really want to live with such uncertainty? Most of us would not. **Insist,** *don't just ask*, that your partner seek help immediately. Tell your partner that until the steps toward recovery are taken, you *will not* get married.

Does my partner humiliate me or put me down in public?

Most of us have parts of ourselves that we are insecure about. It could be some extra pounds or an unequal level of education. Whatever the causes of our insecurities, it certainly does not help to have your partner making even veiled or more openly obvious comments about these insecurities in front of friends or relatives. It might even be less obvious if your partner doesn't say anything, but has a way of making you feel that he or she would rather be with someone else. Unless you let your partner know this behavior is making you unhappy, it is not likely to stop, even after you're married. So make sure you talk this over immediately.

Is my partner too critical?

All of us engage in criticism from time to time. And many of us criticize unnecessarily, usually during an argument. But there is a type of person who seems to find fault with just about everything, including the one they profess to love. This trait exists in both men and women, and it can make life miserable for the person who is a regular target. While some people change after marriage and become more critical of their spouses, most chronic complainers show this side of themselves long before, perhaps in more subtle ways. If you believe your partner is a bit too critical now of "the small stuff," you should make it known you find this behavior unacceptable. If it goes unchallenged, you could be setting yourself up for the verbal equivalent of the Chinese water torture.

Is my partner a compulsive gambler?

There is a big difference between buying an occasional lottery ticket and spending large sums of money on trying to hit the big one. Of course, gambling comes in many forms other than the lottery. Gamblers bet at casinos, horse racing or sports games. And neither gender has a monopoly on gambling addictions.

Does your partner dip into "household" monies just for the thrill of gambling, whatever the game? How much time and money does your partner spend on these activities? Does he or she insist that it's just a hobby? If your partner denies there is a problem, you have to be the strong one. You have to insist that your partner get professional help, or you will end the relationship. This help is freely available to those with or even with "potential" gambling problems through a nationwide organization called "Gambler's Anonymous." Just check your phone book for a local chapter.

Is my partner unreasonably jealous?

The signs, if your partner has showed any, should be clear to you by now. Unwillingness to let you go anywhere by yourself, and a prolonged interrogation when you return. Suspicion of any man or woman you talk to, other than your partner. Constant phone calls when you're alone, just to find out what you are doing at the moment.

Has your partner displayed one or all of these behaviors? If so, it's not a question of being a little over-protective. You might just be dealing with someone who believes "marriage" or a relationship is simply another tool for controlling their partner's life. Assuming you are over the age of eighteen, you do not need anyone's permission to go out on your own. Even if you are living with your partner, you are not a prisoner.

However, you should make sure you are not engaging in behavior that makes your partner question your motives. For example, if you are living together, do you make it a point of telling him or her who you will be seeing that afternoon or evening, and when you expect to return? When you live with someone as a mate, the person is entitled to be treated with courtesy and respect. Are you making sure you do this?

If your partner cannot accept your independence or believe you're not looking to cheat the moment you leave the house, ask yourself what married life with this person would be like. And if that's the kind of life you would really want.

Has my partner broken my trust?

Being able to trust your partner is essential to a happy and successful marriage. When that trust is broken by lying, cheating, verbal or physical abuse, and other hurtful actions, it is difficult to have faith that your partner will not act the same way after marriage. Has your partner ever lied about anything to you in your relationship? What was the reason for lying? Have there been any other times since the first occasion? If a partner makes a habit of lying, you must decide how much this relationship is worth to you. Is it worth the pain?

In a marriage, you do have to learn to forgive, but there is a limit to how much destructive behavior from your partner you should have to take. You should set those limits now, and put any plans for marriage aside until your partner shows that he or she can be trusted again.

Women's Questions

Is he physically abusive toward me?

If the answer is yes, the reasons don't matter. He may have all kinds of elaborate excuses, which may sound plausible to you and make you forgive him. He may even say he loves you, and doesn't know why he hurts you. ***Do not accept any of it!*** A reasonable man who really loves his lady wants to protect her from pain, not be the one to inflict it.

If you truly believe he's capable of changing, you must insist he seek professional help immediately, and keep your distance from him until he does. If you have made any wedding plans, ***cancel them!*** Do not listen to interfering relatives, who may only be concerned about what other people will think. That is not your concern right now. Your health and safety are far more important than the views of those who aren't being abused, not to mention your life.

Should he refuse to consider this, or even deny he has a serious problem, you must leave this abusive relationship without further delay. Too many women have stayed on, hoping for a miracle, with tragic consequences. Statistics show us that far too often this type of relationship results in the death of the woman and not too infrequently, any children within the relationship as well. Don't YOU become one of those statistics.

Is he cheating or flirting with other women?

Men who want to get married should remember that this means "forsaking all others." If the man you are about to marry gives you the impression that he would rather keep the others, he is far from ready for marriage to anyone. He may say things like the other women do not mean anything, but that is ridiculous. If they don't really mean anything, he would not be involved with them.

You could insist that he give up the other women, but odds are you would never know whether he actually did or not, until you start getting mysterious phone calls after you are married. Don't assume that a cheating boyfriend will change into a faithful husband. If he behaves in ways that hurt you, such as flirting with or checking out other women while with you, it might be a good idea to delay wedding plans indefinitely.

"Love is the answer, but while you're waiting for the answer, sex raises some pretty good questions."

(Woody Allen, born 1935)

In-Laws

Either Partner

Do I get along with my partner's parents?

Have you met them yet? Sometimes spouses do not meet their in-laws until after the wedding, and the first meeting is less than successful. Or worse, the spouse discovers the in-laws have decided to dislike him or her for no apparent reason. It would be wise, if you have not already done so, to meet your prospective in-laws before your wedding takes place.

Are they bossy and interfering?

We all like to believe we marry the partner, not the family. For many new husbands and wives, however, this is far from the truth. Meeting your partner's parents and family for the first time isn't easy, and whether you and they will get along is a 50-50 toss-up. Even if you do discover, to your pleasant surprise, that you get along fairly well with them, you might want to get an idea of what their IQ (in their case, it stands for Interference Quotient) score is. If they give you a long list of who should attend your wedding, for example, their potential for interference would be rather high.

It is very important, if they display a preference for meddling in areas that do not concern them, for you and your partner to take control immediately. If your partner seems to be incapable of doing this, after a lifelong habit of giving in to parental pressure, this could spell serious trouble.

How much influence do they have on my partner?

When you consider that they are your partner's parents, this can make an enormous difference in your relationship. Suppose, for some reason, they take a dislike to you. How far will your partner go to back you up? Is your partner strong enough to stand up to the parents and tell them not to interfere?

Observe the way your partner reacts with them by visiting, and not just occasionally. Each visit is your opportunity to gain more knowledge about them and how well–or poorly–they interact. Do they argue more often than you think necessary? If this is the case, does your partner seem to cave in on important issues? Some parents think they are entitled to control their children's lives, even after they marry. If this seems to be the case with your prospective in-laws, you must make it clear to them and your partner that their interference is not acceptable and will not be tolerated.

Friends and Socializing

Either Partner

Do I have to give up my nights out with friends?

It would be unreasonable for your partner to insist that you give up *all* contact with your friends after marriage. However, if you have been going out most nights up to now, you will probably have to make some changes. Your mate, after all, does have a right to ask for the larger percentage of your time.

Happily, this can be worked out with just a little effort. Let us assume you've been going out five nights a week. Would you be willing to cut back to just one night? If you and your partner have no children, you could both have an evening out, with your separate groups of friends, on the same night. And you can determine a time you should both be home. Let each other know where you plan to be, and have the phone numbers of the places handy, in case an emergency comes up. As long as you are considerate of each other when planning nights out with your friends, there is no reason to stop having evenings out alone.

If children become an issue in future, you could still have your evenings out, although not on the same night, obviously. The same rules would still apply; that you tell your partner where you will be, and what time you expect to be home. Promise to call if you are running late, so the partner at home isn't worrying about where you are, or if you are safe. Treating each other with courtesy and respect will help both of you when enjoying evenings out by yourselves.

Remarriage

When marrying for the second time, we have the same issues facing us as in our first, plus a few more. Protecting our children, if any, is our top priority, with consideration for securing our assets, namely money and property, coming in at a close second.

If you have ever read the novel <u>David Copperfield</u> by Charles Dickens, you read how a mother exposed her young son to terrible cruelty and abuse by marrying the wrong man. Although this was fiction, abuse of children is not something we read about only in novels and fairy tales. We also read many horror stories in our news magazines and newspapers. Your children, if you have any, should not only be considered but consulted if you decide to take the step of marriage again. Whom you marry will affect their future too.

Either Partner

Does my partner like children?

If you have never seen the reaction of your partner to children in general and yours in particular, make it a priority to do so immediately. An afternoon or evening spent in a child-oriented environment should tell you what you want to know very quickly. All children, from babies to teens, have ways of pushing the buttons of adults. Some adults have very little tolerance for the typical behaviors they display. There are also adults who have no tolerance at all.

Your children will be directly affected by the choice you make. Naturally, their welfare must take precedence. If your partner shows any hostility toward your kids or seems unwilling to spend time with them, then he or she is not the right partner, for your children or you.

How do my children feel about my partner?

If they are happy that you found someone, you are lucky. Many children and teens feel some degree of resentment toward a new adult coming into their mom's or dad's life. After all, they've probably had your attention focused only on them for some time, and they are not too happy about sharing. This is normal, and should be expected.

However, it might ease the tension if you and your partner schedule activities the children–or teens–enjoy. Make it clear to them that your partner will be included, and they will be expected to be polite, if they can't be friendly. Do not hope for instant acceptance after just one or two occasions. It takes time for such relationships to develop, and trying to rush it for your partner or your children will not make it happen any faster.

There are times when personalities clash, and children will not accept the new partner in their parent's life. It is a very difficult situation, because it may force you to choose. If this is the case, marriage might not be the best course of action right now.

Is my partner hostile to my kids?

Has your partner reacted well to other kids in the past, but seems hostile to yours? If so, find out why. Talk to your kids as well. The worst you can do is nothing, or just assume the problem will magically disappear. Bad relations between your partner and your children could have a disastrous effect on the marriage. Finding the reason for your partner's hostility and taking steps to resolve the problem should be done before you get married.

Am I comfortable with being a stepparent?

Whether your partner has one minor child or more, have you spent enough time with the children as well? This is very important, since you need time to know each other as a family. How do you feel about your partner's methods of discipline? Do you have any feelings of resentment toward them because they take away some of your partner's attention from you? Have you talked about any problems you might have with your partner?

Being a stepparent is not easy, and you must make sure you are emotionally equipped to handle the challenges–and stresses–it will bring. And if you have never had to cope with young children or teenagers before, you are in for a large dose of culture shock. Do not assume any problems will solve themselves after marriage. Those same problems could endanger the marriage if they are not addressed early. Admitting that problems exist can help to work toward an acceptable solution.

However, if you find you cannot easily accept your partner's child or children, even after spending more time with them, it would be a mistake to get married, for all of you.

Am I ready to take this step right now?

You may have reached a point where you've decided life as a single person again, with or without children, is pretty good at the moment. But let us say the person you've been seeing wants something more than a dating relationship. If you would like to continue it without getting married, have a serious talk about it. He or she may agree to postpone marriage indefinitely or may not, and insist you make a decision. It will not be easy, but now you must choose what is more important. If you have any doubts about marrying again at this point, you are better off not going ahead.

A Few Last Thoughts

My father's wedding speech lasted a bit longer than I had requested. "Just five minutes, Dad" were my exact words. But even though he went five minutes over the limit, his final words are still in my mind. In closing, he said, "...and for God's sake, keep your sense of humor. It is indeed one of His greatest gifts, and I don't believe any marriage can succeed without it." Since he was one half of not just one successful marriage, but two, he was definitely on to something.

Would he have thought a book like this was necessary? Maybe not. But things are very different today than they were in the mid-1950's. A sense of humor is still very important in marriage, but a couple should also make it their business to know as much as they can about each other first. The questions in this book are not meant to be easy or fun. They were created to help you think ahead to situations you may never have thought of.

Surprisingly, many couples get married without stopping to consider what life ahead of them might be like. They never take off the rose-colored glasses, believing themselves to be invincible. But, as I discovered personally, bad things do happen. A partner could lose a high-income job. A couple could give birth to a child who has severe medical problems. A partner might be stricken with a terminal illness. Will discussing the questions in the preceding pages *guarantee* a happy and successful

89

marriage? Unfortunately, it can't. However, it would probably give you a better idea of how to handle the challenges you may face after you get married.

There is an old saying: "To be forewarned is to be forearmed." I am not sure of its origin, but the meaning is very clear. Knowing what *could* happen in the future will help you and your partner deal with the events that do. Especially if you can plan ahead.

Having said all I can on this subject, there is only one thing left. Good luck, best wishes, cheers! And save a glass of champagne for me.

Suggested Reading

<u>Marriage</u>

Can This Marriage Be Saved? Real-Life Cases From Ladies' Home Journal, by the editors of Ladies' Home Journal, with Margery D. Rosen

Love Between Equals, How Peer Marriage Really Works, by Pepper Schwartz, Ph.D.

Making Your Second Marriage A First-Class Success, by Doug and Naomi Mosely

Now That I'm Married, Why Isn't Everything Perfect? The 8 Essential Traits Of Couples Who Thrive, By Susan Page

Rock-Solid Marriage, by Robert and Rosemary Barnes

Saving Your Marriage Before It Starts, by Dr. Les Parrott and Dr. Leslie Parrott

The New Couple, Why The Old Rules Don't Work, And What Does, by Maurice Taylor and Seana McGee

We Love Each Other, But...by Dr. Ellen Wachtel

Marriage-Before Getting Married

Before Saying "Yes" To Marriage, 101 Questions To Ask, by Sydney J. Smith

Before You Say "I Do," Important Questions for Couples To Ask Before Marriage, by Todd Outcalt

About the Author

Susan Levine has been a published author since 1997. Following her marital separation in 1999, she began writing this book to help herself through this painful process and with the hope of helping others find marital happiness. The questions presented in her book can help both men and women learn what they need to know about their partners prior to marriage. Answering these important questions prior to marriage can prevent a great deal of marital conflict and distress. Levine lives with her son in Northern Virginia.

Printed in the United States
1483700001BA/66